What Must We Do?

A Blueprint For Releasing God's Power

Larry Huch

FAME Publishing, Incorporated
Coppell, Texas

FAME Publishing, Incorporated
820 South MacArthur Boulevard, Suite 105–220
Coppell, Texas 75019–5574

© 1993 by Larry Huch
All rights reserved. Published 1993
Printed in the United States of America
99 98 97 96 95 94 93   5 4 3 2 1

Unless otherwise indicated, all Scripture quotations are taken from the King James Version of *The Holy Bible*.

Verses marked *(TLB)* are taken from *The Living Bible* © 1971. Used by Tyndale House Publishers, Inc., Wheaton, IL 60189. All rights reserved.

Scripture quotations marked *(NIV)* are taken from *HOLY BIBLE NEW INTERNATIONAL VERSION*. Copyright © 1973, 1978, 1984 International Bible Society. Used by permission of Zondervan Bible Publishers. All rights reserved.

Scripture quotations marked *(NKJV)* are from *The New King James Version*. Copyright © 1979, 1980, 1982, Thomas Nelson Inc., Publishers.

Scripture quotations marked *(NASB)* are taken from the *New American Standard Bible*, © 1960, 1962, 1963, 1968, 1971, 1972, 1973, 1975, 1977 by The Lockman Foundation. Used by permission.

ISBN 1–880563–04–5

What Must We Do?

Now when they heard this,
they were pricked in their heart,
and said unto Peter and the rest of the apostles,
Men and brethren, what shall we do?
Acts 2:37

Contents

Preface ix

Acknowledgments xi

Chapter 1
Do It Again, Lord! 1

Chapter 2
Repent—The First Step Toward God's Power 11

Chapter 3
Be Bold As A Lion 33

Chapter 4
Be Filled With The Holy Ghost 49

Chapter 5
Go Out With A Shout 61

Preface

I was hungry for an answer.

I have always said, "The Bible is not a history book of what Jesus used to do, but a promise book of what He wants to do for His people today."

Why then, are we not seeing the promised outpouring of God's power?

Why aren't we seeing churches bursting with revival? Why aren't Christians living under open heavens in every area of their lives including healing, prosperity, joy and power?

God's Word says it's ours! What's wrong?

Then it hit me!

Jesus says if any of us lacks wisdom, all we must do is ask Him. When things aren't working, if we ask God why, He will reveal the answer. If we'll be honest, the problem always lies in us, never with God or His Word.

All the promises in the Word of God are ours through Christ! Every single one of them.

As a pastor, that means souls for the Kingdom and God's power in the church. Not just a trickle, but a flood.

As a Christian, that means happiness, health and prosperity.

Then, it hit me again! The Holy Spirit was finally starting to get through.

God said, "Larry, there is nothing wrong with My power or My promises. The problem is My people don't understand what's holding Me back. My people are destroyed for their lack of knowledge."

What Must We Do?

God's people are being destroyed in their homes, bodies, finances, marriages, families and churches...not because the devil has suddenly become stronger than God...not because the gifts and power of God passed away with the apostles, but for one big reason: our lack of knowledge.

In the first church service I ever attended, an evangelist called me out and said, "You want everything God has to offer!"

I did then—and I still do now.

Most of you are probably like me, thanking God for what He *used* to do—walls came tumbling down, blind eyes opened, gold coins came out of fishes' mouths, the dead were raised and cities turned to God.

And I know you probably thank Him for what He's *going* to do—streets of gold, crowns on our heads, pearly gates and living forever with Jesus Christ in a place of no tears or sorrow forever!

I hope you understand when I say past and future is not enough.

Jesus is the Lord of *today*. His Word says, "Your kingdom come. Your will be done ON EARTH as it is in heaven" (Matthew 6:10, NKJV).

Jesus really is the same yesterday, today and forever.

He truly is the Lord and changes not.

ALL His promises are to us "yea and amen."

He really meant it when He said, "If any of you lacks wisdom, ask and I will give it to you."

I decided I wanted ALL God had for His people!

My excitement was ignited—I was going to get an answer!

"Okay, Lord, what must we do?"

Acknowledgments

To my wife and best friend, Tiz, who has been here from the beginning. She has been my encouragement and support. Together we pioneered six churches in seventeen years in America and Australia. Every time I said, "Let's do it again," she never lost her spirit or her determination. She has been my encouragement and support. I could not have done it without her!

To Trish Achenbach, my personal secretary, who told me this *had* to be written and continually encouraged me until I did.

To Kathy Hoggard, whose talent and expertise organized and edited my thoughts and notes into print.

1
Do It Again, Lord!

General William Booth ignited a social phenomenon in 1865. It was called The Salvation Army. What began in the dark streets of London spread to the United States, Canada, Europe, Asia, the West Indies, South America, South Africa and to the far corners of the world.

Booth's mission: To usher in the Kingdom of God. He and his followers went into the streets preaching the Word of God, repentance, Jesus Christ and the cross of Calvary. Booth believed repentance and salvation were the only hope for society's redemption.

Thousands responded. People whom the world had given up on were not only saved, but set free from all kinds of bondages. A source quoted in *Christian History* said that The Salvation Army's message was more effective in eradicating crime and disorder in the streets of London than five thousand additional police officers would have been.[1]

This movement erupted in Booth because he began reading the Word of God. As he read what God had done in times past, he became hungry to see those same miracles again.

For many months, on his knees, he begged, "Do it again, Lord. Do it again."

Those who were close to him said all they would ever hear him pray was, "Do it again, Lord. Do it again."

During his life, he journeyed more than 5,000,000 miles and preached 60,000 sermons. Because of his desire to see God again perform the mighty miracles of His Word, Booth's army of believers impacted the world.

Today, in your life, your church and on a worldwide basis, God is getting ready to do it again. He wants to do it again!

But the movement needs to start with you and me!

Those Who Hunger And Thirst Shall Be Filled

Think about what would happen if you had a "Big Mac attack," a real hunger for a big hamburger. I can picture it now.

You jump into your car and drive to McDonald's. A smiling girl comes up to the window and says, "Can I help you?"

"Yeah, I'll have a Big Mac," you reply.

Then she says, "Sorry, we don't have those anymore."

"Well then, give me some fries."

"We don't serve them anymore either," she says.

"How about a Coke?" you say smacking your parched lips.

"We're not serving Coke anymore either," she says still smiling.

"Well, what do you have?" you ask, stomach growling.

She answers, "We have a menu showing what we used to have; we have a menu showing what we're going to have, but we don't have anything right now. You just got hungry at the wrong time."

What a disappointment! The golden arches are still there, but they no longer offer anything to sustain you. Fortunately, this scenario would never happen because we know McDonald's always supplies what's on its menu.

And so does God!

When I read the promises in God's Word, it's clear He is not saying, "Larry, this is what I used to do, but I don't do it any more."

When He shows blind eyes opening; cripples walking; prostitutes, thieves, liars and court officials being saved; He is asking, "Does that make you hungry for revival, signs, wonders and miracles? I am the same yesterday, today and forever. Come and eat."

All His promises are included in the Word of God to whet your appetite. It's all on the menu. He desires to feed His people so much that He's creating within His ministers, including me, a great hunger for the outpouring of His power.

God wants to "do it again!"

Not long ago, I was sound asleep when the Spirit of God woke me. Immediately, the Lord began to fill me with visions of a great outpouring of His power.

People were being saved by the tens of thousands.

Backsliders were coming to the Lord.

Politicians and media people were transformed into strong and vocal Christians.

I saw the power of God being poured out as in the book of Acts. The signs, wonders and miracles following the lives of every true believer confirmed the teachings of Christ.

Armies of young people in love with Jesus were leading their school friends to the Lord. Everywhere, Christians were laying their hands on the sick.

I felt an excitement in my spirit and asked, "Lord, what must we do?"

He answered, "That's what the people asked when I built My first Church; what I told them I am saying again to My last Church.

"To see the Church strong and powerful again, you must remember I, the Lord, change not!"

Follow The Instruction Manual

Recently, I bought a big-screen TV complete with all the latest innovations. According to the salesman, not only could I view what I wanted on one channel, but it had "picture in picture" so I could watch, to my wife's great delight, football and boxing at the same time.

I threw the instruction manual away figuring I could plug the TV in, turn it on, hit a few buttons and everything would work.

Unfortunately, it hasn't been that simple. I haven't been able to use most of the features. I've even attempted to acquire another manual, but the the models have changed. So there my fancy TV sits, not performing to capacity because I don't know how to operate it.

Calling RCA and saying, "Hey, this thing is malfunctioning," is out of the question. Everything to make the technology come alive is sitting in my living room.

That's the way many churches and Christians are. There they sit saying, "God, it's not working."

God replies, "Are you following my instruction manual?"

Not A Good Idea...A God Idea

Did you ever wonder what Jesus meant when He asked, "Do you have eyes but fail to see and ears but fail to hear?" (Mark 8:18, NIV)? He wasn't referring to hearing in the physical sense, but hearing, understanding and acting on the Word of God.

God has a certain way of doing things. Somehow, as Christians we think we can change it and do it better.

The Bible is our instruction manual. It's not a good idea, it's God's idea. Tossing it out and creating something more contemporary will never suffice because God's Word does not change and it will never be out of date! "Jesus Christ [is] the same yesterday, today and forever" (Hebrews 13:8).

Granted, if Jesus came back to earth today in the form of a man, He might alter His ministry slightly. Perhaps He would borrow a car instead of a donkey. Who knows, He might even take a plane. More than likely, He would be healing AIDS instead of leprosy.

The Lord's methods might vary, but who He is, and what He desires to do in the lives of His children, will never change.

God's church, unlike my T.V., operated by His instruction manual will never be obsolete. It's so simple: if we follow The Book, it will work.

"The grass withers, the flower fades, But the word of our God stands forever" (Isaiah 40:8, NKJV).

Build On The Right Foundation

> **Therefore whosoever heareth these sayings of mine, and doeth them, I will liken him unto a wise man, which built his house upon a rock.**
>
> **And the rain descended, and the floods came, and the winds blew, and beat upon that house; and it fell not: for it was founded upon a rock.**
>
> **And every one that heareth these sayings of mine, and doeth them not, shall be likened unto a foolish man, which built his house upon the sand:**
>
> **And the rain descended, and the floods came, and the winds blew, and beat upon that house; and it fell: and great was the fall of it.**
>
> **Matthew 7:24–27**

Any engineer will tell you a building is no stronger than its foundation. As Christians, our foundation is the undiluted Word of God.

God is preparing to again perform mighty miracles, but He needs vessels to work through. He is seeking hearers and doers of His Word. To be used, we must build on the whole Word of God. Don't limit Him by only using the salvation part of the manual and casting the rest aside.

God doesn't care whom He works through. He has chosen the foolish and the willing. Peter reminds us, "God is no respecter of persons" (Acts 10:34). While society makes distinctions among people, God's love, grace and power are available for all.

Do you desire to see God's power manifested in your life? Do you long for signs, wonders and miracles? Is your foundation built on the uncompromised Word of God?

When Jesus healed the two blind men, He told them,

"According to your faith, be it unto you" (Mathew 9:29).
  My Bible says the Word of God changes not.
  My Bible says God shows no partiality (II Chronicles 19:7).
  According to the undiluted Word, my God shall supply all my needs according to His riches (Philippians 4:19).
  My God is a healer, a savior, a deliverer.
  My God raises the dead.
  My God is everything I need Him to be, whenever I need Him to be it.
  Declare the Word of God is true. Declare all God has promised will be reproduced through your life.
  Your foundation must be stable before God will build on top of it. He will not take you to higher levels until you are capable of holding more. Cement your foundation with the full Word of God. Then, He will "do it again." He will pour out His Spirit upon you in a greater way than ever before.
  God isn't looking for polished, professional representatives. He desires people who are pliable—the man, the woman, or the pastor—who will say, "I receive the undiminished Word of God. Here I am, Lord. Send me. I want to be the living fulfillment of Your Word."

Workers Are Few

Then He said to His disciples, "The harvest truly is plentiful, but the laborers are few...."
Matthew 9:37 (NKJV)

It's time for us to quit saying, "God is going to do something," and get up up off the bench and start doing it ourselves.
  It's like football, but on this team, too many Christians are sidelined. Many are injured. Most cut practice. They show up on game day, but they'd rather not get their uniform dirty. God, the quarterback and creator of the game, has already documented all the plays explaining how to win. But, He can't throw a pass unless

there's a receiver running down the field looking to make a catch. It takes teamwork.

We've all heard the adage, "God helps those who help themselves." You won't find this quote in the Scriptures, but it has truth.

God performs the miracles, but we do the work. After a farmer has planted his seed, he needs the miracle of the harvest to take place. God can't perform unless the farmer does his job as well.

We are co-laborers with God.

We must put our hands to the plow.

God has already executed the most important part of the plan. As Jesus Christ hung on the cross He said, "It is finished." He meant that man's redemption had been completed.

We need to quit waiting to see what else God is going to do and start doing our part. God has provided the game plan and the equipment.

It's time for the Church to suit up! God can't "do it again" with most of the team in the locker room.

Time To Wake Up

God is preparing to shake the religious world and set it on fire again. However, He will not move until the Church examines itself. Let's evaluate our walk. Are we on fire? Or has the fire burned down to lukewarm coals? Has the oil in our lamps gone dry?

In the second and third chapters of Revelation, John says FIVE times, "He who has an ear, let him hear what the Spirit says to the churches" (Revelation 2:7, 29; 3:6, 13, 22; NIV).

Don't kid yourself. John didn't have a memory lapse and accidentally repeat himself. On the contrary, John is going all out to warn us about the compromising and lukewarm Church of the last days. Jesus requires absolute devotion. His Word says He will reject lackadaisical followers.

So then because thou art lukewarm, and neither

cold nor hot, I will spew thee out of my mouth.
Revelation 3:16

Zeal for the Lord is not optional. It's time to wake up and prepare for His return. Don't follow in the footsteps of the foolish virgins.

> Then shall the kingdom of heaven be likened unto ten virgins, which took their lamps, and went forth to meet the bridegroom.
> And five of them were wise, and five were foolish.
> They that were foolish took their lamps, and took no oil with them:
> But the wise took oil in their vessels with their lamps.
> While the bridegroom tarried, they all slumbered and slept.
> And at midnight there was a cry made, Behold, the bridegroom cometh; go ye out to meet him.
> Then all those virgins arose, and trimmed their lamps.
> And the foolish said unto the wise, Give us of your oil; for our lamps are gone out.
> But the wise answered, saying, Not so; lest there be not enough for us and you: but go ye rather to them that sell, and buy for yourselves.
> And while they went to buy, the bridegroom came; and they that were ready went in with him to the marriage: and the door was shut.
> Afterward came also the other virgins, saying, Lord, Lord, open to us.
> But he answered and said, Verily I say unto you, I know you not.
> Watch therefore, for ye know neither the day

nor the hour wherein the Son of man cometh.
Matthew 25:1-13

This is not a popular teaching, but the issue isn't that we pastors get you into church. We want to get you into Heaven. I like the old saying, "The Word of God comforts the afflicted, and afflicts the comfortable."

If you are snug as a bug in a rug, you need to get out of your religious rut and into a dynamic discipleship with Jesus Christ. Religion is boring...an ongoing relationship with the living God is not!

I'll never forget the poster hanging in my wife's dorm room in college. It depicted a church entrenched in the doldrums. The preacher looked bored to death, the people looked fatigued, and there was Jesus sleeping in the front pew!

Church, get out of religious ritual and into God's revival! Paul told Timothy to stir himself up (II Timothy 1:6). If your spiritual fire is going out, go back to reading the Word, start praying again, get involved with the powerful things God is doing in these last days.

When we were pastoring our first church in Santa Fe, New Mexico, a youth pastor from another church approached me and said, "Pastor Huch, I've heard about the hundreds of teenagers getting saved in your church. How do you do it? We can hardly get any young people saved, or keep them saved. We've tried volleyball, roller skating, pizza parties—nothing seems to work. How do you do it?"

The Word of God says, "Except the Lord build the house, they labor in vain that build it..." (Psalm 127:1). Pizza is definitely not the answer to keeping youth on fire for God!

Jesus is the Living Water. Living water is moving, going someplace. If water stands still, it stagnates. What was once full of life becomes full of decay. The key to yourself, your church and your youth staying alive is winning souls and continued growth in God. Our efforts are futile without His presence and anointing.

God will not anoint what is lukewarm or compromising. Peter grabbed the attention of the church world on the day of Pentecost by standing up boldly and unashamedly preaching, "Jesus Christ is the Son of God" (Acts 2:36).

This was the same fearful, backsliding Peter, who previously went fishing and took everyone with him. In Acts 2:14-37, Peter is now filled with the Holy Ghost standing up among those who killed Christ, knowing they might kill him too. Unafraid, he is preaching.

My friend, nothing is going to happen in the Kingdom of God, in your life, or in my life until we start moving under the anointing of the Holy Ghost.

Nothing will change by just standing in front of an abortion center or casting our vote on a ballot. It requires much more than this.

When the Church starts moving again under the anointed fire of God, we are going to change the world and turn it back to Jesus Christ. It can start today.

After Peter had preached under the anointing, Acts 2:37 says the people "...were pricked in their heart [they were convicted], and said unto Peter and to the rest of the apostles, Men and brethren, what shall we do?"

It's the same question the Church ought to be asking today, "What shall we do?"

2
Repent —
The First Step Toward God's Power

> Then Peter said to them,*"Repent,* and let every one of you be baptized in the name of Jesus Christ for the remission of sins; and you shall receive the Holy Spirit" (Acts 2:38, NKJV).

As Peter stands preaching under his new anointing, the conviction of the Holy Ghost falls on the entire crowd. They cry out, "Men and Brethren, what must we do?"

I want to point out the question was not, "What must we do to be saved" as is sometimes taught. Salvation comes through the grace of God through Jesus Christ. These people were asking for much more than salvation. They wanted to be Christians with a dynamic walk.

It was a great question then and it's a great question now.

Peter lays it out in three simple steps. Repent, take a stand and get filled with the Holy Ghost.

By following Peter's anointed instruction, the first Church of Jesus Christ was not just born, it burst into existence. On its first day, the church won three thousand lives for Christ and ushered in the mighty acts of the apostles.

Acts says all were in awe of the signs and wonders of the first Church.

New believers were added daily! Multitudes gathered from surrounding cities bringing the sick, the lame and those who were tormented by unclean spirits. The Word of God says, "...They were ALL healed" (Acts 5:16).

Most impressive was the public's response. "The people esteemed them highly" (Acts 5:13, NKJV). The public viewed them favorably! In other words, *The Jerusalem Enquirer* was not running negative exposés on the exploits of the Church.

What was good for the first Church is good for the last Church. As the last Church, we must ask the same question. What must we do—or better yet, what must I do, to see God perform the miracles of Acts again?

First, we must repent!

Repentance is not a word used much in the church today. The Bible tells us to repent, but it means more than saying a little prayer and then going out the door the same way we came in.

To repent means after walking in one direction and living in sin, we receive Jesus Christ, change directions and live in sin no more.

The night I gave my life to Jesus a little Mexican guy invited me to church to see a film called, "The Gospel Road." The end of the movie showed Jesus dying on the cross of Calvary. I was high on drugs. I was an addict and a former drug smuggler, yet I knew Jesus was reaching out to me. I could feel His love all over me.

He didn't say, "Larry, get your act together and then we'll talk." He said, "Come as you are."

Praise God, He took me as I was—no shoes, no shirt and needle marks up and down my arms. But, thank God, He didn't leave me that way. Jesus instantly delivered me from drugs, but I still had a lot of cleaning up to do. It was my responsibility to continue living a life of repentance and change. I had to keep my eyes fixed on Jesus, stay in prayer and be willing to forge ahead.

Church, if ever we needed to repent as a body, it is now!

In some ways, the Church of Jesus Christ has become abusive in its attitude toward God's grace.

"Oh no, Larry!" you may say.

Oh, yes!

Some churches now ordain homosexuals. Some are taking the blood and its power out of the Bible. Others overlook and excuse all kinds of sin.

One reason God has not already poured out His Spirit worldwide is because many Christians have not really repented. My friend, when there is sin in the camp, God has no choice but to judge the whole army.

God is cleaning up the Church.

Many look at the media, who have been exposing sin and corruption in the Church, as persecution from the devil.

I think it's God getting our attention. The unrighteous escapades of the last two decades will no longer be accepted. God is whittling down His army of believers just like He whittled down Gideon's army (Judges 7:2–7).

Before you get too excited about the Lord's chastisement on preachers, remember when He's done with the pulpit, He'll be moving into the pews.

Why is this happening now?

Because the fire of God's power is about to fall and the anointing on His people is going to be accompanied with signs and wonders, many that the world has never seen before. God cannot manifest His power through weekend warriors. He needs soldiers enlisted in His Green Beret army.

Jesus is going to use the same kind of vessels for His last miracles that He used for His first miracle (John 2:1–10). When Mary came to Jesus at the wedding feast at Cana of Galilee and told Him they were out of wine, He didn't say, "Well, just bring me anything and I'll fill it up."

Obviously, there were a lot of empty old "wine skins" laying around, but that wasn't what Jesus wanted. Instead, Jesus said specifically, "Bring me the water pots used after the purification of the Jews." He was going to use clean, sanctified, set–aside vessels for His miracle.

"Jesus is the same yesterday, today and forever" (Hebrews 13:8). No doubt, in these last days He will still only use clean vessels.

You might be thinking, "Larry this sounds kind of harsh. I thought God was a God of love."

He is. More than we can understand. But love means sometimes a father has to say "no" and sometimes it means a spanking, even if we don't like it. That's love.

God cares about His people. He is our Father, and a father chastens the children he loves. "Be zealous therefore, and repent" (Revelation 3:19).

Amazing Grace

If anybody believes in the unmerited, unearned favor of God we have through the blood of Jesus Christ, it has to be me. I came to church that first night high on drugs and walked out high on Jesus.

Giving grace is God's job. Maintaining an ever-repentant heart is ours.

When I was in Australia recently, a pastor who had been caught committing adultery three times stood before his church and excused his behavior by saying, "Folks, I'm only human. The Bible says you must forgive me." He was right. We're all only human and we must always forgive. But the one asking forgiveness also has a part to play.

Forgiveness doesn't include allowing our pastors to get in the pulpit and say, "It's okay for me to compromise. The ten commandments don't really apply to me in this situation." Restoration goes hand in hand with true repentance!

If we as leaders in the pulpit justify our unrighteousness, it gives the green light to immorality in the pews.

John 8:3–11 tells of a woman caught in the very act of adultery. She was obviously guilty. The scribes and Pharisees brought the woman to Jesus in hopes of entrapping Him, not because of a passion for holiness or a desire to restore and set her free. They quoted the law written by Moses, which said adulterers should be stoned and asked Jesus what He thought. Jesus replied, "He that is without sin among you, let him cast a stone at her" (John 8:7).

Then, Jesus stooped down and wrote in the sand. I believe He began composing a list of sins very familiar to the scribes and Pharisees. Her accusers became convicted as their own sin was unveiled. One by one, they split the scene!

> **Then Jesus stood up again and said to her, "Where are your accusers? Didn't even one of them condemn you?"**
> **"No, sir," she said.**
> **And Jesus said, "Neither do I...."**
> **John 8:10-11 (TLB)**

Too often the Church conveniently stops reading right there and says, "Oh, the grace of God covers our sins!"

Sadly, in some cases, the Church has turned God's grace into sin's justification.

Jesus didn't stop by saying, "Neither do I." He continued at the end of verse 11, "Go and sin no more!" In other words, "Don't get religious and act holy. Instead walk in the revelation of a cleansed and purified life."

Jesus prophesied to the "religious" clique two thousand years ago saying:

> **Many will say to me in that day, Lord, Lord, have we not prophesied in thy name? and in thy name have cast out devils? and in thy name done many wonderful works?**
> **And then will I profess unto them, I never knew you: depart from me, ye that work iniquity.**
> **Matthew 7:22-23**

We need to be sure as God's people we don't become

What Must We Do?

modern-day scribes and Pharisees. It's not enough to wear crosses around our necks, pay tithes, carry 40-pound Bibles and prophesy in the name of the Lord.

It's too easy to be like whitewashed tombs, glossed over and beautiful on the outside, lifting our hands and shouting, "Hallelujah," while inside, the sin and corruption of the world still hang on.

Jesus also said:

> **Woe unto you, scribes and Pharisees, hypocrites! for ye are like unto whited sepulchers, which indeed appear beautiful outward, but are within full of dead men's bones, and all uncleanliness.** **Matthew 23:27**

Maybe this is why the world is shouting at us through the media.

Folks, listen to their cry! What they're saying is, "We've tried everything society has to offer and our lives are still empty. Please, keep the Church clean. It's the only place left to go!"

And that's exactly what God is saying to us—

"Get ready!"

"Get clean!"

"The world is about to flood the gates of My house!"

True Christianity requires more than a righteous appearance. We need what happened at the cross in our hearts. The world doesn't need more religion. We need revival. As always, it needs to start with you and me.

Yes, thank God He covers us when we fall and make mistakes. Not only is Jesus *Jehovah-Tsidkenu*, God our Righteousness, He is also *Jehovah-M'Kaddesh*, God our Sanctifier. The blood of Jesus covers and continually cleanses us.

God doesn't require inhuman perfection. On the contrary, His Word says if we make mistakes and ask for forgiveness, it's there every time.

> If we confess our sins, He is faithful and just to forgive us our sins, and to cleanse us from all unrighteousness.　　　　　　　　　　　I John 1:9

Notice the word *if.* Too many times we don't see the condition that comes with the promise. Repentance requires action.

We must confront our weakness so God can make us strong. Maybe we have ignored, justified and swept sin under the rug for too long.

God wants His church clean. He's disinfecting the pulpit and the pew. When the world has had enough of the pig pen, the Father's House must be ready to receive them.

We Can Still Be The Salt Of The Earth

> Ye are the salt of the earth: but if the salt have lost his savour, wherewith shall it be salted? it is thenceforth good for nothing, but to be cast out, and to be trodden under foot of men.
> 　　　　　　　　　　　　　　　　　Matthew 5:13

You are the salt of the earth if you have received salvation and profess to be a child of God through the blood of Jesus at the cross. It doesn't matter whether you are Full Gospel, Charismatic, Baptist, Presbyterian, rainbow people, pink polkadotted, or pinstriped.

You—not just the preacher, or evangelist, or the paid church staff—but YOU. Say it aloud right now, "I am the salt of the earth."

Salt was a substance the Jews understood. It had two purposes. For one, it added flavor to their food. That's why the Psalmist said, "O taste and see that the Lord is good" (Psalm 34:8).

Christianity is the tang in life. God doesn't take away the zest. He lavishly adds to the savor in your life.

If there's one thing I love to tell people it's "Jesus is a Giver, not a Taker!" Christians should be the happiest, healthiest, most–

blessed people on the face of this earth. Jesus said:

> **...I have come that they may have life, and that they may have it more abundantly.**
> **John 10:10 (NKJV)**

Secondly, salt acted as a preservative. Long before General Electric and refrigeration, it kept perishables from rotting.

Jesus likens us to salt because we are to guard and protect the world from spoiling. As salt, we must rescue decaying souls permeated with sin and despair.

However, salt also has its drawbacks. It's easily polluted. Barnes tells us when it loses its preserving power, the taste of whatever it touches enters into the substance of the salt.[1] If it touches onions, it tastes like onions. If it touches meat, it tastes like meat. Polluted salt takes on the flavor of what it should be protecting. As Christians, if we're not *affecting* the world, the world will start *infecting* us!

Salt isn't pure by nature either. In Jesus' day, miners used great care to separate earthly substances from the salt. Knowing this, Jesus said if salt is mixed with the earth (the world), it loses its power and is good for nothing but to be thrown down and used like gravel (Matthew 5:13).

It's no wonder the world is walking all over the Gospel of Jesus Christ! The Church has become contaminated with society's value system.

The Word of God says,

> **Wherefore come out from among them, and be ye separate [from the world], saith the Lord, and touch not the unclean thing; and I will receive you.**
> **II Corinthians 6:17**

Based on God's Word, the morals and lifestyle of Christians should be considerably higher than the world. However, when society's ideals began to deteriorate, the Church allowed its morals to fall as well.

The fluctuating mores of any given culture should never be embraced by the Church. We are the salt—the preservative, the flavor—we are to penetrate the world!

It's the old frog-in-the-pot story all over again! If you put a frog in a pan of lukewarm water and slowly turn up the flames, the frog won't notice the gradual change in temperature. He'll stay there until he dies.

Can you feel the heat?

It's time to jump out of the devil's pot and back into the river of living water!

Restoring God's People

It's been said that the Christian army is the only army in the world that kills its wounded. In the last few years, we've seen leaders in the front lines of the Church fall. The enemy has aimed for and hit a few of our generals. But what Satan has meant for evil, God will turn into good. Remember the Word of God says, "...All things work together for good..." (Romans 8:28).

You might be asking what possible good could come from leaders falling. But the Church can learn from these mistakes. If we'll love these men and do all we can to restore our brothers, they will be greater men of God.

Even David and Peter, to name just a couple, failed. But they turned their hearts back toward the Lord and He restored them. They went on to do great things for God!

Like Christ, we need to nurture back to a healthy walk with Jesus those who have been hit by the enemy's sword. We need to love one another!

The #1 Sin In The Church

When the Lord began to speak to me on how He is preparing

to open the windows of Heaven on His people, He said, "Larry, this is the number one reason My Church has not seen anywhere near all that I have for them."

The Lord revealed to me that the primary reason we have not yet seen God's best is because of whispering, backbiting and gossiping in the Church of Jesus Christ.

I believe we can conquer this giant and take the next step toward God's power:

> **And even as they did not like to retain God in their knowledge, God gave them over to reprobate mind, to do those things which are not convenient.**
>
> **Being filled with all unrighteous, fornication, wickedness, covetousness, maliciousness; full of envy, murder, debate, deceit, malignity; whisperers,**
>
> **Backbiters, haters of God, despiteful, proud, boasters, inventors of evil things, disobedient to parents,**
>
> **Without understanding, covenant–breakers, without natural affection, implacable, unmerciful:**
>
> **Who, knowing the judgment of God, that they which commit such things are worthy of death, not only do the same, but have pleasure in them that do them.**   **Romans 1:28–32**

Sounds like a description of a group to avoid! Unfortunately, as Christians, disassociation could be difficult because God is talking about His people!

This same chapter says these people "knew God." In other words, they were aware of God's existence and understood His call to righteousness. Yet, they deliberately rejected His ways.

We have a tendency to think unrighteousness only includes sleeping around, drugs, and other "terrible things." Actually, there's no such thing as big or little sin. Sin is sin. We need to repent of it all.

Too many Christians are not only involved in gossip and backbiting, but they don't even realize the impact it's having on their church and on their lives.

> **Being filled with all unrighteousness... wickedness, covetousness, maliciousness; full of envy, murder, debate, malignity, whisperers.**
> **Romans 1:29**

We know murder is a sin. Fornication, yep, that's a sin too. Fornicators, haters of God—oh, those dirty sinners!

But take another look. God names whispering, backbiting and gossiping in the same group. These are some of the most damaging sins in our churches today.

These are the ugly sins of viciousness toward one another. It's the kind of talk that says, "Check out that woman over there! Look at the way she dresses."

Isn't it interesting that God put envy, murder and whisperers right next to each other?

Do you know what a whisperer is?

Have you ever gotten a call from Sister Sounding Brass or Brother Tinkling Cymbal saying, "I'm just calling to ask you to pray about this..." and then the caller proceeds to pass along harmful gossip about another in the church? Let's face it folks, this is sin!

Do you think it's a coincidence that "backbiters and haters of God..." stand linked in the scriptures? Why would God place these two sins in unison? What message is He sending to His people?

God clarified His intentions when the disciples asked, "Lord, what is the greatest of Your commandments?"

Jesus answered saying, "That you love one another."

What Must We Do?

Love God And Love God's People

> **A new commandment I give to you, That ye love one another; as I have loved you, that ye also love one another.**
>
> **By this shall all men know that ye are my disciples, if ye have love one to another.**
>
> **John 13:34–35 (NKJV)**

During the first three years of our ministry in Portland, Oregon, we watched our church, New Beginnings Christian Center, skyrocket from 10 to 3,000 people. Because of the phenomenal growth, many frequently asked me, "Why do you think this is happening?"

Obviously, it was the grace of God, but in addition, God said I must not allow two things in our church. One is gossip and the other is competition with any other church in town. The day I'm jealous of another pastor is the day it's obvious I'm building *my* kingdom, not God's.

I absolutely know we must first love one another before we will see God manifest His power in our churches.

This area of repentance by the Church of Jesus Christ is one of the most crucial points in this book.

It's not only crucial for you, but for the unchurched world as well. Jesus said, "All men will know that you are my disciples if you love one another" (John 13:35, NIV).

Notice Jesus didn't say, "They'll know you're My disciples because of your big buildings and dynamic programs."

The world won't know who we are until they see true, Godly love in the midst of us.

We need God's guiding principle of love at the forefront of ALL our relationships. Only then will the church catapult into the arena of irrefutable evidence of transformation and new life in Jesus Christ!

These Two Are The Same

> Then one of them...asked him a question...saying,
> Master, which is the great commandment in the law?
> Jesus said unto him, Thou shalt love the Lord thy God with all thy heart, and with all thy soul, and with all thy mind.
> This is the first and great commandment.
> And the second is like unto it, Thou shalt love thy neighbor as thyself.
> On these two commandments hang all the law and the prophets.   Matthew 22:35–40

Jesus again alerts us to the importance of love in our relationships!

First, notice again the word "commandment." Loving God and one another is a command, not a suggestion. In other words, it's more than a hint from God.

Second, it's impossible to have love for God and hate for others in your heart. These two emotions are juxtaposed in the Kingdom of God. They repel each other. It's contrary to God's Word to say you love the Lord and harbor ill feelings toward a brother or sister in the church, a co-worker, a family member, or your neighbor across the street.

> If a man say, I love God, and hateth his brother, he is a liar: for he that loveth not his brother whom he hath seen, how can he love God whom he hath not seen?
> And this commandment have we from him, That he who loveth God love his brother also.
>   I John 4:20–21

What Must We Do?

Again, He reiterates love is a commandment. We are to love God and people—*these two are the same.* According to the Word, loving God and people is a package deal. You can't choose to love one and not the other. If you profess love for God and speak ill of another, you are a liar. Now, don't get mad at me. I didn't say it. God did! As a Christian, it's impossible to say good things about God and slander others.

When I became a Christian I made a decision to stop doing drugs. I also chose not to drink alcohol anymore. In comparison, we can also choose not to gossip, backbite, hate or be envious. It's a decision God has called us to make. Through His power, we can be set free from every sin.

Love can be more than a meaningless motto. It can become a lifestyle!

Blessed Is The Peace Maker

A pastor from another state recently called because he was worried over reports of discord in the body of a nearby church. He wanted to know what to tell his congregation and members from the other church who began filtering over.

"You need to tell your congregation, it does not matter what they've heard or how true it is. They need to pray God intervenes and all damage will be repaired."

When a fracture occurs in the Body of Christ, too often Christians are like buzzards, swarming around waiting for the corpse to die so they can pick the bones.

James addressed breakdowns in the Church of Jesus and asked, "Why is there war and fighting amongst us?"

Fortunately, he didn't leave us without an answer...

> **From whence come wars and fightings among you? come they not hence, even of your lusts that war in your members?   James 4:1**

Personal jealousies and selfishness are the spirits behind gossip and slander. Sometimes we think God must be stupid. We call a friend specifically for the purpose of gossiping, but think God won't notice because we disguise the gossip by passing it off as a need for prayer or a deep concern.

Come on folks! Do we really think we can pull one over on God?

No way! He knows the intent of our hearts.

Gossip and slander are the hidden cancers killing the Body of Christ. Not only is it ungodly, it's stupid. Listen to this:

Be ye not deceived; God is not mocked: for whatsoever a man soweth, that shall he also reap.
Galatians 6:7

The Law Of The Harvest

God's law of the harvest says we reap what we sow. If the Church plants seeds of gossip, the Body will reap disunity and become a dysfunctional family. If the Church sows love, the Body will respond by growing into a powerful coalition.

I'm convinced this is the main reason God's people are not seeing His best in their lives—the main reason so many of their own problems grow all the time. Jesus said:

...The kingdom of God is like a man who casts seed upon the soil;
and goes to bed at night and gets up by day, and the seed sprouts up and grows—how, he himself does not know.
Mark 4:26–27 (NASB)

If we desire money, God says, "Sow money." If we want friends, be friendly. If we want peace, plant seeds of peace. Remember, "Blessed are the peacemakers..." (Matthew 5:9). I don't know about you, but I want to be marked by God's favor. If we want to be blessed, we must repent of any of these sins in our lives. Say this out loud right now so it's planted deeply in your heart, never to be forgotten: "I will reap what I sow."

It's time for us to wake up and start planting good seeds!

Unity In The Body

For I received from the Lord that which I also delivered to you: that the Lord Jesus on the same night in which He was betrayed took bread;

and when He had given thanks, He broke it and said, "Take eat: this is My body which is broken for you; do this in remembrance of Me."

In the same manner He also took the cup after supper, saying, "This cup is the new covenant in My blood. This do, as often as you drink it, in remembrance of Me."

For as often as you eat this bread and drink this cup, you proclaim the Lord's death till He comes.

Therefore whoever eats this bread or drinks this cup of the Lord in an unworthy manner will be guilty of the body and blood of the Lord.

But let a man examine himself, and so let him eat of that bread and drink of that cup.

For he who eats and drinks in an unworthy manner eats and drinks judgment to himself, not discerning the Lord's body.

For this reason many are weak and sick among you, and many sleep.

I Corinthians 11:23–30 (NKJV)

Let's go over a few of these verses, so the Holy Spirit can show you what He's shown me about the Body of Christ. First, let's look at verse 26:

> **For as often as you eat this bread and drink this cup, you proclaim the Lord's death till He comes.**

When we take the Lord's supper we are proclaiming, "Jesus has died for us. He took my place. I'm a Christian." Remember, to be a Christian means to be Christ-like. Now look at verse 27:

> **Therefore whoever eats this bread or drinks this cup of the Lord in an unworthy manner will be guilty of the body and blood of the Lord.**

God says don't eat in an unworthy manner or we are guilty of the body and the blood of the Lord. I don't know about you, but that verse used to confuse me because none of us are worthy. God is our righteousness and He is continually working on all of us.

Then the Holy Spirit gave me one of the greatest truths of my life. If you're a pastor, this will change your church. If you're a Christian, get ready for the windows of Heaven to open up!

Look at verses 29 and 30:

> **For he who eats and drink in an unworthy manner eats and drinks judgment to himself, not discerning the Lord's body.**
> **For this reason many are weak and sick among you, and many sleep.**

First, it says if we eat and drink in an unworthy manner, judgment is released on us. Bad news! Then it says, for this reason many are sick and dying. Look around:

Churches are sick and dying!
Ministries are sick and dying!

People, finances, families and marriages are sick and dying! Why?

God gave us the answer and I never saw it.

For *this* reason many are sick among you!

What reason, Lord?

He answered, *"For not discerning the Lord's body."*

The word *discerning* means "not giving proper treatment to" the Lord's body.

Folks, God's not talking about reaping judgment or being cursed over a little piece of bread. The body He's talking about treating right is sitting beside you in church every week!

> **For as the body is one and has many members, but all the members of that one body, being many, are one body, so also is Christ.**
>
> **For by one Spirit we were all baptized into one body—whether Jews or Greeks, whether slaves or free—and have been made to drink into one Spirit.**
>
> **For in fact the body is not one member but many.**
>
> **Now you are the body of Christ, and members individually.**
> **I Corinthians 12:12–14, 27 (NKJV)**

We are the Lord's body. When we gossip and backbite we are closing the windows of Heaven over our lives.

We are cursing ourselves.

As if that weren't enough, the Word of God says every time we hurt one of God's children, we are persecuting Jesus. When Paul was on the road to Damascus Jesus asked:

> **…Why are you persecuting Me?**
> **And he said, "Who are You, Lord?" And the Lord said, "I am Jesus, whom you are persecuting…."** Acts 9:4–5 (NKJV)

Paul had never even seen Jesus. But the Lord still asked, "Why are you persecuting *Me*."

When we touch one of God's children, we are touching Jesus! The Word of God also says when we do something to the least of our brothers, we do it to the Lord (Matthew 25:40). In other words, Jesus was saying, "When you do it to them, you do it to Me!"

You may say, "Lord, I never saw and understood this before. I didn't realize what You meant about discerning Your body."

The Lord replies, "I know. Now, go and sin no more!"

Folks, even though God is still working on various areas of our lives, there is one commandment we can *choose* to follow today.

Love one another!

Remember the old adage, "Like father, like son"? When we show love, mercy and kindness, who are we mirroring? When we backbite, slander and act in hate, who are we representing?

It's a pretty simple question.

Think about it.

Like father, like son.

Which father are you imitating?

Breaking Down The Barriers That Divide

The law of the harvest and God's commandment that we love one another apply to more than just the dynamics among the members of any given church. It also pertains to the interrelations of one whole church to another church body.

All throughout the world, a very exciting thing is happening: walls are coming down. This tearing down of barriers is a miracle of God. The Berlin Wall, the Iron Curtain, communism, and barriers in Romania and many other eastern block countries are being demolished.

In the same way, walls of division among churches must come down before we'll see the outpouring of God's Spirit. This includes denominational walls!

Now, don't get all excited until you hear me out. If you're Assembly of God, be proud of that; if you're Baptist or another denomination, be proud too. Nothing is wrong with joining a group. However, it's a crime when belonging to one set of Christians separates us from other Christians.

Now, I know you're thinking, "But we believe differently." Let me respond by quoting Paul.

> **For I determined not to know anything among you, save Jesus Christ, and Him crucified.**
> **I Corinthians 2:2**

Do you believe Jesus was born of a virgin, died on the cross, shed His blood for the forgiveness of sin, rose again on the third day, is the only begotten Son of God, and that through no other name we can be saved? If you do, then we are brothers in Christ Jesus. Doctrine is important, but not to the point of causing division.

I don't believe any of us understand the Word of God completely. We're all doing the best we can. Although the Bible is without flaw or contradiction, the Holy Spirit moves through imperfect earthen vessels. Some day we're all going to have a big laugh when we stand before Jesus and He says, "Come here, Larry. Let Me show you what this scripture *really* means."

> **For now we see through a glass darkly; but then face to face: now I know in part; but then shall I know even as also I am known.**
> **I Corinthians 13:12**

As long as we profess Jesus as our Savior, no doctrine is worth dismembering the Body of Christ.

Church, we must repent. When God touches our hearts, it's never to condemn, only to convict. He tenderly nudges us so we can be closer to Him.

It's time for the Church to truly become the salt of the earth and penetrate the world. We can start by tearing down the walls of division between our brothers and sisters in our own congregations and among all the churches in the Body of Christ. Let's take the first step of Peter's advice. If we repent, we will build up a holy army, take the world for Jesus and usher in the signs, wonders and miracles promised to us in the Word of God!

3
Be Bold As A Lion

Then Peter said to them, "Repent, and let every one of you *be baptized in the name of Jesus Christ for the remission of sins*; and you shall receive the gift of Holy Spirit" (Acts 2:38, NKJV).

Peter's second instruction to the first Church was "be baptized in the name of Jesus Christ for the remission of sins." That is, be baptized in water.

Peter was talking to a group who needed courage to make a public stand. When a Jew chose to follow Christ's teachings and be water baptized in the name of Jesus, he was making a public declaration.

Many times this meant loss of inheritance and being shunned by family. Parents would say, "We have no son," or "Our son is dead." It was an immense step of boldness for a Jew to be baptized in water.

Let's look again at the second chapter of Acts:

> Now when they heard this, they were pricked in their heart, and said unto Peter and to the rest of the apostles, Men and brethren, what shall we do?
> Then Peter said unto them, Repent, and be baptized every one of you in the name of Jesus

Christ for the remission of sins, and ye shall receive the gift of the Holy Ghost. Acts 2:37–38

Examine this carefully because it is one of the most misquoted portions of scripture in the Bible. Again, let me explain, the people did not ask what they must do to be saved. Their question was open ended. They wanted to be saved—but beyond salvation they desired to have a Christian walk like Peter.

According to the scriptures, to be saved we need only to repent and receive Jesus.

Water baptism does not save us.

Speaking in tongues does not save us.

Going to church and raising our hands doesn't save us.

Neither does wearing a cross save us.

Only one thing can redeem us: the blood of Jesus.

We are saved when we believe in the Lord Jesus Christ, repent of all sins and accept His blood as a cleansing of those sins. We are not saved through our works or meaningless ritual.

Peter told them after they received salvation, they *needed* to be baptized in water. Now let me help you understand something. No power exists in the ritual of being dunked in or sprinkled with water. The power lies only in the revelation of God's Word.

Satan's greatest trick is to take the Word of God and turn it into insignificant ritual.

Why do some people baptize babies when no teaching in the Word of God instructs us to sprinkle infants?

It's a ritual the church has adopted even though according to the Word of God, baptism is for those who have accepted Jesus Christ as their Lord and Savior.

Baptism is a revelation of the death of the former life and the resurrection of new life in Christ Jesus. When we are baptized, we are submerged in the water. When we arise, we are boldly proclaiming our stand in Jesus Christ!

What was required of the first Church for a dynamic walk with the Lord is imperative for the last Church. Peter's instructions

to the first Church were:
- Get saved—receive Christ as your Savior. Don't just say a prayer; repent of your sins.
- Make a stand—don't become a closet Christian.

The need for boldness is nothing new. Often we place the men and women from the Bible on a pedestal as though they were superstars. We should love and admire their walk with God, but we need to remember they confronted the same battles you and I face. If they could win the battle of intimidation, we can too.

Even Paul the apostle confronted fear. When he was in prison awaiting trial he wrote to the church at Ephesus asking them to pray that God would give him words, so he might open his mouth and boldly proclaim the revelation of Jesus Christ (Ephesians 6:19). As an ambassador for Christ, he realized the need for unreserved utterance and candor.

We are all Christ's ambassadors.

The men and women God has called as teachers and leaders in the Body of Christ, and the multitudes of Christians who fill the pews in this century, must also make a new declaration!

It's time for a new freedom of speech.

It is our right in Jesus to be bold!

God's System Of Government

The attack may come from many fronts, but Satan's attempt to keep Christians muzzled is nothing new.

I cover this next part only to encourage and stimulate. My purpose is to lift up God's leaders and release the Church into a new dimension.

Satan wholeheartedly desires to keep pastors and teachers timid when it comes to preaching the Word of God. Even Satan knows boldness must start in our leaders! If the Church wants smoke in the pews, there must be fire in the pulpit.

Flames will burst forth in the pulpit and ignite the pews when

What Must We Do?

God's leaders stand up against every demonic spirit that would keep them as ambassadors in chains.

The Apostle Paul was imprisoned in the physical sense. He was shackled and confined. In our day, too many pastors and leaders are shackled spiritually.

The Church of Jesus needs to rally around her leaders the same way the church of Ephesus supported Paul in prayer when he needed boldness. It takes courage for God's leaders to implement His system of government.

Sometimes church people boast, "I've been in the way for ten years," meaning they've been serving Jesus for a decade. The unfortunate truth is many literally have been *in the way*: a hindrance to their pastors.

It's time for church members to stop blocking the path and freely allow God's leaders to do what God is calling them to do.

Don't misinterpret! I absolutely believe in accountability. My life, my beliefs, my morals and my finances are an open book. I am accountable to a board of pastors and I have a board of deacons in my church whom I trust and love.

But in God's system of government, God first calls a man and the man picks a board. If you have a board totally controlling a man called by God, you've got it all wrong. The ministry is not a job. It's a calling.

I had lunch with a pastor who told me his board showed up at his house and said, "We've decided you're not needed any longer." He started another church, and the same thing happened again—politics.

"What do I do?" he asked me.

"Make a stand. Tell them you won't have manipulation in God's House."

"But if I do, I'll lose some of the people," he said.

As a pastor, I would rather have fifty people standing with me than five hundred surrounding me.

The cry needs to change from, "Pharaoh, let my people go" to "People, let my pastors go!"

A pastor's battle cry must be, "Follow me."

The Hireling Or The Shepherd

The thief cometh not, but for to steal, and to kill, and to destroy: I am come that they might have life, and that they might have it more abundantly.

I am the good shepherd: the good shepherd giveth his life for the sheep.

But he that is an hireling, and not the shepherd, whose own the sheep are not, seeth the wolf coming, and leaveth the sheep, and fleeth: and the wolf catcheth them, and scattereth the sheep.

John 10:10–12

The thief in this verse is often assumed to be Satan. Really, it's just the devil in disguise. If you look closely, this scripture is actually referring to the hireling or the false shepherd. Many of God's shepherds have become hirelings. Some by choice, others by force.

We live in a day when pastors are quitting by the droves. Telling people the good news ought to be fulfilling. Why are many of God's men and women checking out and moving on?

Recently, I was driving down the highway in another state where I was scheduled to speak. We passed a huge, beautiful church. I asked about it and was told it was extremely popular and successful. Attendance ran into the thousands. Unfortunately, one Sunday morning the pastor got up and said to the congregation, "I quit."

He left the ministry and went into business.

Why?

Because even though he loved and served God, his congregation wore him out. It wasn't the work of the ministry, but the politics of the people.

It's time for pastors and leaders to get BOLD and be the men God called them to be, not the men the Board tells them to be.

"Peter, Lovest Thou Me?"
"Yes, Lord."
"Feed My sheep."

Christianity is simple. We're the ones who have made it complex. We've transformed it into a buffet. We pick out what we feel like eating and don't touch the rest. Our pastors and leaders, who have been called to serve, are often pushed to dish up only what the congregation feels like digesting.

Jesus didn't invite us to a spiritual smorgasbord. He's planned a perfect four-course meal.

When growing up, Mom made you eat the nutritious stuff before giving you dessert. Remember Grandma? She always gave you what you wanted when you wanted it.

Too many pastors are trying to be Grandma, squirting whipping cream by the truckloads into the congregation, while the green beans are getting colder by the minute.

Don't misunderstand: the Gospel of Jesus Christ is packed with whipping cream, but if you want the body to work, you've got to eat everything on your plate.

Without a healthy spiritual diet, we become vulnerable targets for spiritual diseases.

If because of the power of "noise, nickels and numbers," (attention, money and crowds) we let people be whatever they want to be and live as they wish, without warning them of the danger, we are hirelings. In other words, we're afraid if we preach the truth, we'll lose people.

A recent *Time* magazine featured a lead article entitled, "The Church Search." The article talked about the baby boomers coming back to God, but on *their own* terms.[1]

Church leaders are called to feed God's sheep, not to tell people what they *want* to hear—instead, to tell the congregation what they *need* to hear.

As a pastor with a growing church, I get books and tapes on "How To Build A Church For Today's Generation." Many of the tapes advise, "Don't preach on sin, money or commitment, if you want to draw a crowd."

It's true, you will draw a crowd, but will you be setting them free and preparing their souls for an eternity with Christ?

Despite the topics contemporary experts on church growth may suggest as crowd pleasers, the Bible still says, "Repent." That means pastors need to tell their churches to stop living in sin. The Bible still says a tenth is the Lord's and offerings besides. That translates into a bold message on sowing and reaping. God still requires total commitment.

True Christianity requires faithfulness, accountability and leaders who are not afraid to boldly declare the *whole* Word of God.

The Enemy Has A Strategy

As Christians, we need to remember we are at war. Look at what else Paul says to the church at Ephesus :

Put on the whole armour of God, that ye may be able to stand against the wiles of the devil.
Ephesians 6:11

Paul says to put on the armor of God so we can stand against the wiles of the devil. Armor is for soldiers and it's crucial in battle. It's not so we can look good walking around the parade ground.

The word *wiles* means "methods or strategies used in an attempt to destroy." One of Satan's most effective strategies is to embarrass us for being Christians. This attack comes from a wide range of sources.

Let a Christian leader fall and it's smeared on the front page of every newspaper and magazine in the country. Entertainers mock those who are born again. Movies like "Leap Of Faith" portray Christians as being crazy, fanatics and con men.

This is not new.

Jesus was mocked. But He never backed down.

Neither must we.

We have nothing to be embarrassed or ashamed of. On the contrary, through Jesus Christ we have the answer to all life's questions. Turmoil of every kind permeates the streets, schools, nations, marriages, and our personal troubled minds, but Jesus is the Prince of Peace, *Jehovah-Shalom*, the Calmer of Storms. He is the Healer of all diseases: AIDS, cancer, diabetes, heart problems, sickness of every kind. "...With his stripes we are healed" (Isaiah 53:5).

Jesus isn't a rich-man's God or a poor-man's God; He's not a white-man's God or a black-man's God; He's the God of "Whosoever shall call upon the name of the Lord shall be saved" (Romans 10:13).

I remember a commercial on TV showing a little girl swinging in the park. A black child passed by, then an oriental child, a child from India and so on. Finally the little girl asked, "Mommy, what color is Jesus?"

"Jesus, is the Light of the world," the mother answered, "and pure light is made up of every color in the rainbow."

Everyone deserves to hear the life-changing message of Jesus Christ. We are ambassadors to the world! We must proclaim our message boldly.

I Am Not Ashamed

> **For I am not ashamed of the gospel of Christ: for it is the power of God unto salvation to every one that believeth; to the Jew first, and also to the Greek.   Romans 1:16**

Paul had to fight against the strategy of being ashamed more than once. He had great standing in the Jewish community before he began hanging around with a ragtag group of "religious nuts." But Paul's experience on the road to Damascus wasn't an act of religion; it was an encounter with the resurrected Son of God.

Remember your first encounter with Jesus? Recall how you felt when He came into your heart and forgave all your sins? Remember what it felt like to be born again?

Go for that feeling again.

Get the fire burning and start sharing it with others.

Paul said, "I'm not ashamed of the gospel of Christ," that means the *whole* Gospel. It covers everything that the shedding of His blood bought back for us at the cross.

All that we lost in the first Adam was regained through the Second Adam when He shouted, not from sorrow and defeat but with power and victory, "IT IS FINISHED!"

Jesus said if you're ashamed of Him, He is going to be ashamed of you when He returns. This means you need to be bold for Jesus. You have to stand for God. He is your King.

Peter and the other disciples took their stand on the day of Pentecost and proclaimed, "Men and brethren, you killed the Messiah; but if you repent..." (Acts 2:29–38, paraphrased).

God's not asking you to die for Him; He just wants you to live for Him every day and everywhere you go. It's time to stand up and be counted.

Evidence Of Boldness

Now when they saw the boldness of Peter and John, and perceived that they were unlearned and ignorant men, they marvelled; and they took knowledge of them, that they had been with Jesus.
Acts 4:13

What was the evidence these men had been touched by the Son of God? What was the evidence these men had been washed in the blood? What was the evidence these men had sat at the Master's feet?

Their boldness!

They weren't ashamed!

They weren't selling out. They weren't going to bow down, slow down, or bend down. They were bold, proud and willing to live for Jesus.

Jesus can't use secret agents or Lady Clairol Christians, where only God knows for sure. He needs front–line warriors!

While pastoring our first church in New Mexico, we were invited to bring one of our Christian bands into the Santa Fe Prison for a fourth of July celebration. Fifteen or twenty other groups were supposed to perform as well. However, that spring, the inmates rioted and several people were killed. Tension still existed among the inmates and the media said the prison was a potential powder keg.

When we got to the prison we were surprised to discover we were the only group who had shown up. Our band was small, non-professional and knew about ten songs. We prepared to play for a hostile, captive audience.

The band played its repertoire of ten songs.

Another man and I preached. We weren't nervous; we were scared stiff. When we asked those who wanted to receive Jesus to come up front, dozens came forward—young men, old men, whites, blacks, Hispanics.

Afterwards, as we talked with the men, one Christian inmate said, "Pastor, see all those guys who asked Jesus into their hearts? Well, it may cost them their lives. They might be killed by the others for becoming Christians."

"Do they know this?" I asked.

"Yes, but they've chosen to make a stand for Jesus."

Later, I was standing in the prison yard talking with some of the men when the crowd became quiet and started to spread apart.

Walking toward me was a man who looked like he had come off a movie set for "Hell's Angels." He was the one blamed for stirring up the riot in the prison. He stood in front of me and said five words I'll never forget.

"Preacher, I've been watching you...." Then he said, "You live what you preach, don't you?"

"Yes, sir, I do. Jesus is very real to me."

Then this hard, tattooed inmate asked the most important question in the world, "Will Jesus forgive somebody like me?"

"All you have to do is ask."

So right there, in broad daylight, in front of everybody, Satan lost again. This "lifer" knelt in that prison yard and by the grace of God, this convict became an "eternal lifer!"

When I look back, I realize it had little to do with talent, skill, or the ten songs played by the band. It had a lot to do with BOLDNESS.

It took resolution for the band to go into the prison, bravery for those men to come forward, and courage for that one man to pray in front of the rest.

We all need to stand for Jesus. Your stand may not be in a prison, but you can stand in your school, on your job and in your neighborhood.

Remember those words, "Preacher, I've been watching you." Others are looking at your life. They desperately want to know if Christianity is real. They may laugh, mock, cuss and fuss, but they're hurting and need to see Jesus in us. The world is waiting for the answer.

One of the biggest lies Satan ever released is that Christians are a bunch of sissy weaklings.

Folks, Jesus was no weakling.

He was the lion of Judah!

And He says to us right now, "Follow Me. Be like Me. Gentle as a lamb, but bold as a lion!"

Go Ye—He Means You

And He said to them, Go into all the world and

preach the gospel to every creature.
Mark 16:15 (NKJV)

Jesus gave the Church a great commission: He wants us to go into all the world and preach the Gospel to every creature. The Gospel is Jesus Christ. It's the salvation message, but it includes casting out devils, raising the dead, and healing the sick. As Christians we are to be witnesses for Jesus in Oregon; Washington; Texas; Washington, D.C.; New York; the Philippines; Guam; China; Russia—in all the world.

Do you know what the word *witness* means? It means "one who testifies and has personal knowledge of."

You are testifying and representing Jesus to others.

The Bible tells us Jesus is with us wherever we go. "...Lo, I am with you alway, even unto the end of the world..." (Matthew 28:20). So go, "Heal the sick, cleanse the lepers, raise the dead, cast out devils: freely ye have received, freely give" (Matthew 10:8). The Word of God clearly says He will confirm His Word among those who boldly go forth declaring the power in the name of Jesus!

We often lament over the condition of the world and pray, "Do something."

The Lord replies, "I'm trying."

"Send somebody, Lord."

God says, "I'm trying."

"Who are You going to send, Lord?"

And the Word of God says, "*You* go and preach the gospel to every creature!"

These creatures include those you work with, family and in-laws. Make a stand! Be proud!

Tell somebody about Jesus today. He really is the Answer. Make a stand for Him and watch the change in your life as He begins to stand for you.

I still remember the first time I made a stand for Jesus. Three weeks prior, I had been a drug addict, a dealer and a smuggler.

Then in a moment of time Jesus came into my life and set me free. Shortly thereafter, a visiting evangelist prophesied that I had a call from God on my life to preach, but at three weeks old in the Lord, I still hadn't won any souls to the kingdom.

Then, one night a friend of mine came up and said, "So, you're going to preach."

"Yes," I said, "I believe I am."

"Do you love Jesus?" he asked.

"Yeah, I really do."

"Are you ashamed of Him?" he asked.

"No."

"Fine," he said. "Meet me tomorrow morning downtown. You and I are going to stand on the corner and preach Jesus."

All of a sudden I went, "Oh, God."

See, it's one thing to lift your hands in the church and say, "Thank You, Jesus. Glory to God. Bless you, brother. Hallelujah!" But it's quite another thing to do it among the Philistines.

All that evening, I pictured myself wearing a robe, walking in sandals, carrying a sign that read, "PREPARE TO MEET THY DOOM."

All night long I prayed for the rapture, an earthquake, sickness—anything to keep me from having to preach on the street. But morning came.

You know what I was experiencing because you get the same feeling when the Holy Ghost says, "Hey, you know that guy at work who's having marital problems? Why don't you tell him about Jesus?" Or when you're walking down the street and the Lord says, "Look at that biker over there. Why don't you tell him what Jesus did in your life?"

The next day my friend and I met at Four Corners, the busiest intersection in Flagstaff, Arizona.

It was Saturday morning; the traffic was terrible; people were walking all over the place. There were no songs, no tracts, nothing to get you in the mood.

Suddenly, my 300-pound, freckle-faced, red-headed friend

got up on the car and said, "I'm here to tell you about a Man who died on the cross to set captives free."

I was thinking, "Oh, my God! Oh, no. I have died and gone to hell!"

But in my heart, I knew his message was right on.

To my dismay, my friend's voice finally went hoarse. He turned to me and said, "Okay, now you go."

I jumped up onto the car and said, "Jesus loves you. He loves me, and He loves you; He loves those cars; He loves this light post...."

I have no idea what I said, but I said it loudly.

I didn't know Genesis from Revelation, or one denomination from another, but I did know Jesus Christ loved me. I knew He had accepted me as I was and had come into my heart and changed my life forever.

All of sudden, a normal-looking man came up to me and said, "Man, I need what you've got. Would you pray with me."

I turned to my friend and said, "Hey, I've got one!" And I've been winning souls ever since.

Develop A Burden For Souls

For whosoever shall call upon the name of the Lord shall be saved.

How then shall they call on him in whom they have not believed? and how shall they believe in him of whom they have not heard? and how shall they hear without a preacher?

And how shall they preach, except they be sent? as it is written: How beautiful are the feet of them that preach the gospel of peace, and bring glad tidings of good things!
Romans 10:13–15

Jesus needs ambassadors who will boldly proclaim, "You must

be born again." He needs a Church who will tell the world the good news. How else will the guy at work ever know about Jesus?

Many years ago I began to study the difference between the ministries that had made a powerful impact and those that had been just a flash in the pan.

Smith Wigglesworth had a dynamic ministry until the day he died at the age of 87. I asked the Lord, "Why was it so powerful?"

It was because Wigglesworth preached the Word of God until he died. He never stopped loving souls or bringing people to Christ. On the day of his death, when he was an old man, he preached his last sermon, sat down and went to be with Jesus.

Many churches don't give altar calls anymore. They've fallen out of love with souls.

Christians won't witness just because they're supposed to; nor will they pray or read the Word of God because they ought to. We will only witness and get into the Word of God because the desire is burning inside us!

Have you ever noticed when Jesus touched someone, He would say to them, "Now don't go tell anybody?" But as soon as Jesus left, they went and blabbed to everyone.

"Lord, what is this? Are they all rebels?" I asked.

"No!" He said, "When you are touched by Me, you can't keep your mouth shut."

Lord, give us a fresh touch!

We need a fresh touch from Jesus.

We need the power of God.

We can do thousands of crusades, see all kinds of people healed, and all kinds of miraculous events, but if people aren't saved, we're not fulfilling The Great Commission (Matthew 28: 19–20).

Years ago a man asked me, "If you wanted to convince people to get saved, what would you do?" One of the brothers with me said, "Man, I would let someone spend ten minutes in Heaven and he would get saved."

Another of the brothers replied, "I would let him spend ten

seconds in hell, then he would get saved."

We need a vision of Heaven, but we also need a vision of hell; we need to realize where the world is headed if the Church doesn't fulfill its commission.

Winning the world for Jesus has to start with us.

What must we do?

Repent!

Be baptized.

Make a stand for God. Get bold.

Are you making a stand for God? If the answer is "yes," then keep it up. But if the answer is "no," start right now. Pray this prayer:

> **Father, forgive me for being afraid or ashamed. I rebuke that spirit of fear and receive boldness to share the good news of Jesus Christ. I want God by His Spirit to release boldness upon my life right now. Amen.**

Next, make a stand for Jesus. God will challenge you tomorrow or the next day. He may show you somebody at work, school, the gas station or the mall, who needs a touch from Jesus.

Like the first Church, we too are a group who need courage. When Peter told the first Church to be baptized in water, He was suggesting much more than a meaningless dip in a nearby lake.

He was revealing the secret of a dynamic walk. He was releasing another key to unleashing signs, wonders and miracles.

When you make a stand for the Lord, He will make a stand for you. He will confirm His Word!

Give us boldness, Lord! The last Church of Jesus Christ is ready to make a stand!

4
Be Filled With The Holy Ghost

> Then Peter said to them, "Repent, and let every one of you be baptized in the name of Jesus Christ for the remission of sins; *and you shall receive the gift of the Holy Spirit.*
> "For the promise is to you and to your children, and to all who are afar off, as many as the Lord our God will call." Acts 2:38–39 (NKJV)

After Peter told the first Church to repent and take a stand, he instructed them to be filled with the Holy Ghost.

Many of us in the last Church of Jesus Christ have been taught the Holy Ghost passed away with the apostles. Some Christians don't believe the infilling of the Holy Ghost exists as a separate experience. Others have been told it's still available, but only for a select few.

According to the Word of God, if you have accepted Christ as your Savior, you have answered the Lord's call—and the infilling of the Holy Spirit is promised unto YOU!

Scripture demonstrates it is both a separate experience from salvation and available to ALL God's Children.

John the Baptist prophesied about the forth-coming gift of the Holy Spirit:

> I indeed baptize you with water unto repentance: but he that cometh after me is mightier

> than I, whose sandals I am not worthy to carry:
> He shall baptize you with the Holy Ghost, and fire.
> **Matthew 3:11 (NKJV)**

When John the Baptist was preaching in the wilderness of Judaea he prophesied saying, "There is one who is coming after me who will baptize you in the Holy Ghost and fire."

He understood the baptism of the Holy Spirit was a distinct experience with life-changing evidence.

Paul also realized the Holy Ghost was a separate experience from salvation. When ministering after the departure of Christ, he asked believers if they had been filled with the Holy Ghost:

> **And it came to pass, that, while Apollos was at Corinth, Paul having passed through the upper coasts came to Ephesus: and finding certain disciples,**
>
> **He said unto them, Have ye received the Holy Ghost since ye believed? And they said unto him, We have not so much as heard whether there be any Holy Ghost.**
>
> **And he said unto them, Unto what then were ye baptized? And they said, Unto John's baptism.**
>
> **Then said Paul, John verily baptized with the baptism of repentance saying unto the people, that they should believe on him which should come after him, that is, on Christ Jesus.**
>
> **When they heard this, they were baptized in the name of the Lord Jesus.**
>
> **And when Paul had laid his hands upon them, the Holy Ghost came on them; and they spake with tongues, and prophesied.** **Acts 19:1–6**

Paul asked Christians if they had received the Holy Spirit. When he laid hands on them, the Holy Spirit came upon them.

They spoke with tongues and prophesied.

Although they were already followers of Christ's teachings, Paul saw the necessity for a second experience.

In addition, this fire of God is never described as falling on a selected few. On the day of Pentecost, the Bible says ALL who were present received:

> **And when the day of Pentecost was fully come, they were all with one accord in one place.**
>
> **And suddenly there came a sound from heaven as of a rushing mighty wind, and it filled all the house where they were sitting.**
>
> **And there appeared unto them cloven tongues like as of fire, and it sat upon each of them.**
>
> **And they were all filled with the Holy Ghost, and began to speak with other tongues, as the Spirit gave them utterance.** **Acts 2:1–4**

When Jesus walked the earth, He spoke of the purpose and power of the Holy Ghost. Look at the passage He read publicly at the synagogue in Nazareth from the book of the Prophet Isaiah:

> **The Spirit of the Lord is upon me, because he hath anointed me to preach the gospel to the poor; he hath sent me to heal the brokenhearted, to preach deliverance to the captives, and recovering of sight to the blind, to set at liberty them that are bruised.** **Luke 4:18**

Then Jesus closed the book and said, "...This day is this scripture fulfilled in your ears" (Luke 4:21).

Jesus was saying, "I am here to execute ALL that is in the Word of God. The anointing of the Holy Ghost is upon me—to preach the Gospel, to heal and to deliver.

The Bible is a book of prophecy, not a history book. God

doesn't tell us about gold coins coming out of a fish's mouth, the blind receiving sight, the cleansing of lepers, the raising of the dead and the deliverance of the demon possessed to get us all excited, only so He can inform us that He doesn't do this anymore.

The Bible is not about what God used to do; it's a book about what God wants to do for and through us today.

Only He can save us, but when it comes to deliverance and healing, Jesus said:

> **...Peace be unto you: as my Father hath sent me, even so send I you.**
> **And when he had said this, he breathed on them, and saith unto them, Receive ye the Holy Ghost.**   **John 20:21-22**

Jesus commanded us to receive the Holy Ghost because He is the power of God working in and through us. Look at the change in Peter. In a moment of time, he went from a man who would deny he even knew Christ, to preaching salvation to the very ones who took the Lord's life!

Church, Jesus Christ is the same yesterday, today and forever. The only difference between His promises of two thousand years ago and today is that He is manifesting them through us. As the Father sent Jesus, now Jesus is sending us.

The Devil Will Fight It

The devil will resist the baptism of the Holy Ghost more than anything else in your life other than salvation.

He breaks out in an unholy sweat every time a believer gets filled with the Holy Ghost.

Satan knows something many Christians are not aware of.

The Holy Ghost is a Power Source!!

The father of all lies has invented a monstrosity of falsehoods since the day of Pentecost. His lies have convinced much of the

Church that the baptism of the Holy Ghost is unavailable to them. As always, Satan's lies are contrary to the Word of God.

Prior to ascending into Heaven, Jesus left us one last commandment. Jesus knew He was going back to be with His Father. The message of Jesus would shortly be left in the hands of all His disciples, present and future. He knew our flaws and weaknesses, and prescribed the formula for success that we would need after His departure from earth!

> **And, being assembled together with them, commanded them that they should not depart from Jerusalem, but wait for the promise of the Father, which, saith he, ye have heard of me.**
> **For John truly baptized with water; but ye shall be baptized with the Holy Ghost not many days hence.** **Acts 1:4–5**

The Purposes Of The Fire—The Power

Jesus told us the Holy Spirit equals power. In *Strong's Concordance,* *power* in the Greek is the word *dunamis*, which means "miraculous power, ability, abundance, might, strength, violence, mighty works."[1]

In *Webster's Collegiate Dictionary* the words *dynamo* and *dynamite* come from the same Greek word *dunamis*.[2] Jesus said, "I'm going to give you dynamite power to do the work that I have called you to do." Look at what Jesus told the disciples:

> **But ye shall receive power, after that the Holy Ghost is come upon you: and ye shall be witnesses unto me both in Jerusalem, and in all Judaea, and in Samaria, and unto the uttermost part of the earth.** **Acts 1:8**

Now you can see why the devil fights the Holy Spirit. For

starters, he doesn't want you to get saved; but if you do, he wants to keep you religious, not full of dynamite power.

When you receive the baptism of the Holy Spirit, you receive God's Spirit in you, working for and through you. You become dynamite for God.

After you take a stand for God, the Holy Spirit also gives you a divine enabling to be bolder than ever before:

> **And now, Lord, behold their threatenings: and grant unto thy servants, that with all boldness they may speak thy word,**
>
> **By stretching forth thine hand to heal; and that, signs and wonders may be done by the name of thy holy child Jesus.**
>
> **And when they had prayed, the place was shaken where they were assembled together; and they were all filled with the Holy Ghost, and they spake the word of God with boldness.**
>
> Acts 4:29–31

Personal Power

Many Christians don't like to admit it, but when we get saved, we're not always immediately set free from every bondage.

When I gave my life to Christ, I was born again; Jesus came into my heart and I felt Him forgive my sins. I walked out of church a child of God. However, I was still bound by violence. Something else needed to happen in my life.

It's inadequate to tell new converts or struggling brothers and sisters to "just say no." We need to empower them with the *ability* to say no.

I was sick of being violent.

I wanted to quit losing control of my temper.

I didn't need someone to *tell* me to quit. I needed someone to *help* me quit.

That someone was the Holy Spirit!

A man laid hands on me two weeks later and I received the baptism of the Holy Ghost with the evidence of speaking in tongues. From that day, I've been free from those brutal eruptions.

The baptism of the Holy Ghost did not save me. Jesus Christ saved me. Yet, it was the indwelling of the Holy Spirit who consumed me to such a degree that I had no room for Satan's temptations. The Holy Ghost gave me the personal power to say *no* to the world's lifestyle.

He gave me first-strike capability. No longer was I on the defense waiting to see what vice Satan would lure me with.

Instead, I was invading Satan's ground.

The Power Of Signs

The Holy Ghost is also the manifestation or the "handwriting on the wall" to the world that Jesus is the Christ.

The Bible guarantees in these last days God will confirm His Word with signs, wonders and miracles.

The devil aspires to shut down the Holy Ghost because he hates to see Christians manifest God's power. Signs confirm to the lost that Jesus Christ is who we say He is—the Son of God.

> **Do you not believe that I am in the Father, and the Father in Me? The words that I speak to you I do not speak on My own authority; but the Father who dwells in Me does the works.**
>
> **Believe Me that I am in the Father and the Father in Me, or else believe Me for the sake of the works themselves.**
>
> **Most assuredly, I say to you, he who believes in Me, the works that I do he will do also; and greater works than these he will do, because I go to My Father.   John 14:10–12 (NKJV)**

What Must We Do?

Several years ago I went to the Philippines for a crusade. The first three nights, sixty thousand people heard our message. Ten thousand people received Christ as their Savior. Miracles took place and Jesus was greatly glorified.

A few days later, we arrived on another island where the people had never heard the Gospel of Jesus Christ. Many had never seen a white man before.

The music began and a crowd gathered, but when we walked up on the stage, the people ran into the darkness. The plaza emptied.

We sang.
We worshiped.
We preached.
We invited them to come forward and receive Jesus.

Instead of thousands responding, two or three timidly walked to the front.

We had nothing to lose and everything to gain. I announced, "Now, we're going to pray for the sick. Jesus our Savior is also our Healer. He wants to heal your body."

We prayed by faith for healings. After a long silence, out of the darkness a man started walking across the plaza, carrying a large rag. It looked like half of a bed sheet and was soaked in fresh and dried blood. He climbed up on the platform and one of the Filipino pastors interviewed him.

The man took the microphone and said to the people lurking in the shadows, "You all know me. I was a walking dead man. I came here tonight to find out if this Jesus really is the Son of God. And if He was, would He heal me. Look at me, I am healed. I am healed! Come, Jesus is real!"

People began swarming out of the shadows by the thousands. What we couldn't do with our music or preaching, Jesus did through one skinny Filipino. God demonstrated Jesus Christ really is His Son by confirming His Word with a miracle.

During the next three nights, the crusade was packed. People were saved by the thousands and healed by the multitudes.

We later received a letter from the mayor of the island inviting us to return. The entire village had accepted Christ!

This was the manifestation of the power, the *dunamis*, the dynamite, the fire of the Holy Ghost!

Unleashing the power of the Holy Ghost allows God to freely confirm Himself.

While we were pastoring in Australia, one of our ministries was to the drug addicts who lived on the surrounding streets. We had been trying for months to win these people to Jesus with little success.

Our young people would preach and share Jesus. The addicts would gather to listen, but not respond.

One night as one of our young men was standing on a bench sharing about Jesus, someone threw a wine bottle at him. Everyone but him saw it hurtling through the air. As the bottle neared the side of his head, it stopped mid-air, froze for a moment, and fell to the ground without touching him. The street people were amazed. Fifty-eight of them came to church that night and gave their lives to the Lord.

We asked why they had finally come. Each of them said, "Because we saw the power of God demonstrated."

People need to see the power of God!

John's Faith Needs A Boost

Even John the Baptist himself was assured Jesus Christ was the Lord through signs.

> **And it came to pass, when Jesus had made an end of commanding his twelve disciples, he departed thence to teach and to preach in their cities.**
>
> **Now when John had heard in the prison the works of Christ, he sent two of his disciples,**
>
> **And said unto him, Art thou he that should**

come, or do we look for another?

Jesus answered and said unto them, Go and shew John again those things which ye do hear and see:

The blind receive their sight, and the lame walk, the lepers are cleansed, and the deaf hear, the dead are raised up, and the poor have the gospel preached to them. Matthew 11:1-5

Prior to going to prison, John the Baptist had been crying in the wilderness preparing the way for the Lord. When Jesus walked out into the river to be baptized, John declared without a doubt, "Behold, the Lamb of God."

But while in prison, questions began bombarding his mind. I think he wanted to be absolutely positive the man he was willing to die for was the Christ; so he sent his disciples to Jesus and asked, "Are You the one?"

Look at Jesus' answer, His confirmation: "Go and tell John the things that you both see and hear. The blind receive their sight, the lame walk, the lepers are cleansed, the deaf hear, the dead are raised up, and the poor have the gospel preached to them."

Jesus answered John's question by saying, "Here's the proof of Who I am." God said, "I will confirm My Word. I will prove My Word with signs, wonders and miracles."

This is why the Church needs the Holy Ghost, why the devil fights the Holy Ghost and why Jesus commanded us to receive the Holy Ghost!

I want to speak to those who are saved, but have never received the baptism of the Holy Ghost. I also want to speak to those who have received the Holy Ghost, but have let that river of living water dry up within you. You need to get filled or re-filled with the power, fire and dynamite of the Holy Ghost. If you want that fire, that dynamite, that purging, that power living in you, pray with me right now:

Holy Spirit, fill me to overflowing. Fill me with Your cleansing power. Fill me with Your dynamite power. Lord, I want to lay hands on the sick. I want to pray for people and see them delivered. I want to be used by God in these last days. I want to let people know we serve a resurrected God, a God of power, and a God of strength. In Jesus' name. Amen.

The Holy Ghost is your spiritual muscle. Too many Christians spiritually resemble PeeWee Herman. Jesus intended us to look like a spiritual Arnold Schwarzenegger.

The more you use your muscle, the stronger it becomes. Build it up!

Use it in prayer.

Use it in praise.

Use it every day.

When you get up each morning ask the Lord to refill you, because we are leaky vessels. Lay hands on people so they can see and feel the power of the living God.

Don't be ashamed of the Holy Spirit and His power.

Never allow any board, any pressure, or anyone talk you out of releasing the Holy Ghost in your church.

Remember, it is God the Father, God the Son, and God the Holy Ghost.

God will do it again! But first we must repent, take a stand for Him and get filled with the Holy Ghost!

God wants to bring another spiritual explosion into His Church. When dynamite ignites, everybody knows it. Things move and change. It's time to detonate the dynamite in our lives again, through receiving the Holy Ghost. The world needs evidence of our living God! Receive Him!

Receive the dynamite. Receive the fire!

We live in revival days; just let God be God in your life.

Then you will see signs, wonders and miracles!

5
Go Out With A Shout

And it shall come to pass in the last days, that the mountain of the Lord's house shall be established in the top of the mountains, and shall be exalted above the hills; all the nations shall flow unto it.

And many people shall go and say, Come ye, and let us go up to the mountain of the Lord, to the house of the God of Jacob; he will teach us of his ways, and we will walk in his paths: for out of Zion shall go forth the law, and the word of the Lord from Jerusalem.

And he shall judge among the nations, and shall rebuke many people: and they shall beat their swords into plowshares, and their spears into pruning hooks: nation shall not lift up sword against nation, neither shall they learn war anymore.

Isaiah 2:2-4

Church, listen to what the Prophet Isaiah is saying about you and me! He is describing the last Church!

The Bible says the *mountain* of the Lord's house—not gutter, not valley, not rut, not sink hole—shall be established on the *top* of the mountain. That means exalted above everything else—above every principality, government, power and disease.

Isaiah is telling us in the last days the Lord's House is a mighty mountain looking down on the devil's measly mole hill.

It says the nations will flood to Jesus. That means China, America, Africa, Russia, India and every nation bound in darkness will see revival! That includes salvation for drug addicts, gang members, government officials, the Senate and the House of Representatives. Black and white will not rise up against one another, and God's people will stand in one accord.

The last Church is going to see a movement of unity on earth before the rapture. People are going to say, "Let's go serve God!"

We look around society and say, "Pornography, drugs, alcohol, AIDS and gangs. It's so bad." But where sin abounds, God's grace abounds more! The world is running out of things to try! The world is looking for the answer!!

Read the powerful response of the Church prophesied by Isaiah:

> **So they shall fear the name of the Lord from the west, and His glory from the rising sun; when the enemy comes in like a flood, the Spirit of the Lord will lift up a standard against him.**
> **Isaiah 59:19 (NKJV)**

If you go back and read this verse in the original translation, it doesn't say the enemy comes in like a flood. It says, when the enemy comes in, *like a flood God will raise up His standard among His people.*

Folks, when a flood comes in, you can sandbag all you want, but there's no stopping it.

The last Church will embrace the undiluted Word of God. Then Isaiah tells us we will rise up against sin and the enemy, unstoppable and triumphant!

> **My people are destroyed for their lack of knowledge.** **Hosea 4:6**

Too often God's children get wiped out in battle because of

inadequate learning about the Word and ways of God.

Put into context of the last days, this means if half of all Christians have visions of death and beheaded martyrs, Satan's goal of defeating the Church has been made 50 percent easier!

Many Christians adhere to the doctrine of persecution, envisioning the Bride of Christ going out with a limp and a moan.

Scripture upon scripture has been wrongly interpreted to convince the Church that she will be imprisoned and persecuted unto death.

Most doom and gloomers use Luke 21 as proof of persecution to the Church prior to the rapture. The verses below, often applied to the Church, are actually describing two different events both occurring after the rapture.

In Luke 21 verse seven, the disciples ask what signs will accompany the last days. Jesus says before the very end there will be earthquakes, famines and pestilence and:

...They will lay their hands on you and persecute you, delivering you up to the synagogues and prisons, and you will be brought before kings and rulers for My name's sake. Luke 21:12 (NKJV)

This verse refers exclusively to the persecution of Israel during the tribulation. The Word says nations will rise against nations, kingdom against kingdom. Israel will be persecuted, trampled and eventually turn to God.

The scriptures go on to say Jerusalem's destruction is imminent when she is surrounded by armies. Men's hearts will stop in fear of the future. However, the next verse says:

Then they will see the Son of Man coming in a cloud with power and great glory.
Now when these things begin to happen, look up and lift up your heads because your redemption draws near. Luke: 21:27-28 (NKJV)

Verse 27 says the Lord will appear in the clouds with power and great glory. In other words, He's going to be making an entrance! Here, Jesus is alluding to the second coming, which occurs seven years after the rapture.

Remember, when the rapture occurs, the Church will be gone in the twinkling of an eye. In these verses, He is addressing those who did not receive Christ prior to the rapture.

The bottom line is, God doesn't care if you believe in pre-, mid- or post-tribulation. Any of us may be wrong. The real issue is to be like the five wise virgins and have your vessel full of the oil of God. If you do, when the Groom comes for the Bride, you'll be ready.

Regardless of when Christ comes for His Church, God's army is not going out defeated!

We're going out in victory, with a shout of triumph!

The Hundredfold Blessing On The Church of Jesus

Assuredly, I say to you, there is no one who has left house or brothers or sisters or father or mother or wife or children or lands, for My sake and the gospel's,

who shall not receive a hundred fold now in this time—houses and brothers and sisters and mothers and children and lands, with persecutions—and in the age to come, eternal life.

But many who are first will be last, and the last first. **Mark 10:29-31 (NKJV)**

This verse is referring to the only kind of persecution the Church of Jesus Christ will ever see!

Jesus says in THIS TIME His people will receive a hundredfold blessing. As God pours out His Spirit, there's going to be anointing, blessing, power and abundance on the Church.

I had always struggled with the meaning of the teaching, "many who are first will be last, and the last first" (Matthew 19:30), until God clearly showed me that He is speaking about a *reverse of power* in the world, in the government, in our schools and on our streets! The Church of Jesus Christ will be on the mountain top taking dominion!

Who was it that persecuted Jesus in the Bible? It wasn't the world and it wasn't the sinners.

It was the Pharisees!

The Pharisees were worried about Jesus because of the MULTITUDES following Him!

In these last days, the Pharisees are already rising up and attacking the power in the blood of Jesus Christ. Everywhere we go, people are attacking men and women who are preaching the undiluted Word of God.

Look at what will happen if the Church backs down from the whole Word of God. The scriptures say we will miss the thirty, sixty and hundredfold blessing of God:

> **"Therefore hear the parable of the sower:**
> **"When anyone hears the word of the kingdom, and does not understand it, then the wicked one comes and snatches away what was sown in his heart. This is he who received seed by the wayside.**
> **"But he who received the seed on the stony places, this is he who hears the word and immediately receives it with joy;**
> **"yet he has no root in himself, but endures only for a while. For when tribulation or persecution arises because of the word, immediately he stumbles.**
> **"Now he who received seed among the thorns is he who hears the word, and the cares of this world and the deceitfulness of riches choke the**

word, and he becomes unfruitful.

"But he who received seed on the good ground is he who hears the word and understands it, who indeed bears fruit and produces: some a hundredfold, some sixty, some thirty."

Mathew 13:18–23 (NKJV)

The thirty, sixty, hundredfold blessing of God coming to the Church includes financial success, signs, wonders, miracles and the outpouring of God's Spirit on all flesh!

The Church won't be persecuted from preaching that Jesus is the Savior. The Pharisees will rear their heads when the Church rises up in power and says,

Jesus is the Healer!
He's the Prosperer!
The Deliverer of devils!
Jesus Christ is the same yesterday, today and forever!
He's a big God!
He's a multiplying God!

Persecution will arrive packaged in the same way it has always been. Religious on the outside. Heretic hunters on the inside, jealous of the power and the anointing of Jesus Christ.

The world didn't persecute Jesus! For the most part, they embraced Him.

As God pours out His Spirit, the Church will become a living manifestation of the signs, wonders and miracles of God.

The Pharisees will attempt to squelch the fire of God. But signs and wonders in these last days will convince a lost and dying world Jesus is truly the Christ!

It Has Always Been God's Pattern

And Elijah came to all the people, and said, "How long will you falter between two opinions? If the Lord is God, follow Him; but if Baal, then follow

him." But the people answered him not a word.

Then Elijah said to the people, "I alone am left a prophet of the Lord; but Baal's prophets are four hundred and fifty men.

"Therefore let them give us two bulls; and let them choose one bull for themselves, cut it in pieces, and lay it on the wood, but put no fire under it; and I will prepare the other bull, and lay it on the wood, but put, no fire under it.

"Then you call on the name of your gods, and I will call on the name of the Lord; and the God who answers by fire, He is God." So all the people answered and said, "It is well spoken."

I Kings 18:21-24 (NKJV)

We're nearing the 21st Century and people still don't know who to follow. All kinds of religions, all sorts of gods scream for their attention.

Elijah faced the same problem. The people were stuck between who was really God. Was it the Lord or Baal? Elijah said, "Let the god who answers by fire be God." The people agreed.

The prophets of Baal cried out all day, cutting themselves until blood gushed from their bodies.

Elijah built his altar, drenched it with water three times and called out to the Lord in verse 36 saying, "Let it be known this day that You are God."

The fire of God not only fell, it consumed the sacrifice, the wood, the stones, the dust and licked up the water.

The people saw the power of God and declared, "The Lord, He is God." They fell on their faces and a great revival broke out in the land.

These were not people in rebellion. They were torn between two opinions. They weren't against God; they just didn't know who He was!

It's no different today. The world is still confused. Society doesn't care what name is plastered on the front of our buildings. When they see the fire of God, when they see God is a Healer; a Deliverer; a Mender of marriages; a Breaker of bondage; the Answer to cancer, leukemia and AIDS; when they see God answer by fire, they will say, "This is the God of all Gods," and we'll see revival in the land.

Signs, wonders, and miracles are not the keys to salvation. God just uses them to prime the pump.

This Biblical pattern of showing Himself occurs repeatedly in both the Old and New Testaments. Look what Jesus said in the New Testament:

> **And these signs will follow those who believe: In My name they will cast out demons; they will speak with new tongues;**
>
> **they will take up serpents; and if they drink anything deadly, it will by no means hurt them, they will lay hands on the sick, and they will recover."**
>
> **So then, after the Lord had spoken to them, He was received up into heaven, and sat down at the right hand of God.**
>
> **And they went out and preached everywhere, the Lord working with them and confirming the word through the accompanying signs. Amen.**
>
> **Mark 16:17–20 (NKJV)**

God says He will give the message of salvation validity. He'll remove any doubt by manifestations of authority and indisputable fact.

The supernatural confirmations following Christ's disciples didn't cease in the New Testament. In fact, Acts is the only book in the Bible without an ending. We are the present–day fulfillment of the book of Acts. Signs and wonders can't be limited to past generations any more than God's commission that we preach the gospel.

Jesus said, "Blessed is he who is not offended because of Me" (Luke 7:23).

Who is Jesus?

He's our Savior!

Strong's Concordance explains the meaning of *salvation*, which comes from the word *Sozo*. It means sanctified, healed, delivered and complete.[1] Jesus represents much more than redemption from sin.

He was saying blessed is he who is not offended of speaking in tongues, signs, wonders and miracles!

Blessed is he who is not offended of raising the dead, healing the sick and casting out devils!

Enticing words and eloquent debate won't win the world to Jesus. Paul learned that lesson early in his ministry when he preached in Athens at the Areopagus, a forum in the city for discourse.

Paul debated eloquently. He was an educated man. A scholar! Yet the Bible says only a few were saved. In other words, it was pretty weak!

Paul's next sermon in Corinth wasn't intellectual or philosophical. He shared his testimony and told about his life-changing experience with the living God on the road to Damascus. His testimony was affirmed with signs, wonders and miracles, and MULTITUDES were saved!

Later Paul says, "And I, brethren, when I came to you, did not come with excellence of speech or of wisdom declaring to you the testimony of God..." (I Corinthians 2:1).

He goes on to say, "And my speech and my preaching were not with persuasive words of human wisdom, but in *demonstration* of the Spirit and of power" (I Corinthians 2:4).

Paul was telling the people, "Hey, I didn't come here to talk you into something. I came to tell you Jesus Christ is the Son of God and to allow Him to manifest His Spirit in power through me!

Time and time again people received the teachings of Christ

because they saw Him and His disciples back up the Word of God. They saw undeniable power!

John 6:2 says a great multitude followed Jesus BECAUSE they saw His signs which He performed on those who were diseased!

Multitudes came to the Lord in the Old Testament when they witnessed supernatural manifestations.

Multitudes received Christ in the New Testament when Paul and the apostles laid hands on the sick, healed the lame and the blind!

Multitudes are still halted between two opinions, wondering who God is!

Today, multitudes will still flock to Jesus when they see Him confirm His Word!

It's no wonder the devil tries to stop God's people from laying hands on the sick!

No wonder the devil attempts to tell God's people that signs, wonders and miracles passed away with the apostles!

Jesus told His disciples, even if they didn't understand all of His teachings or understand who He was and what He represented, that they could believe because they had seen the signs, wonders and miracles!

Believe Me that I am in the Father and the Father in Me, or else believe Me for the sake of the works themselves.

Most assuredly, I say to you, he who believes in Me, the works that I do will he do also; and greater works than these he will do, because I go to be with My father. John 14:11-12

His Power Working Through You

Jesus told us He was going to be with His father. Before departing He said, "Where ever you go, tell them the Kingdom of

Heaven is here. Heal the sick, raise the dead, cause the blind to see and the deaf to hear."

"Tell them Jesus Christ is here."

"I will go with you and confirm with signs, wonders and miracles!" Church—God is getting ready to do it again!

What must we do?

We must repent!

We must take a stand!

We must get filled with the Holy Ghost and Fire!

Thirty Seconds To Midnight

On the same day Peter told the people to repent, take a stand, and get filled with the Holy Ghost, he quoted the prophet Joel:

> **And it shall come to pass in the last days, says God,**
> **That I will pour out of My Spirit on all flesh;**
> **Your sons and your daughters shall prophesy,**
> **Your young men shall see visions,**
> **Your old men shall dream dreams.**
> **And on My menservants and on My maidservants**
> **I will pour out My Spirit; in those days;**
> **And they shall prophesy.**
> **I will show wonders in heaven above**
> **And signs in the earth beneath:**
> **Blood and fire and vapor of smoke.**
> **The sun shall be turned into darkness,**
> **And the moon into blood,**
> **Before the coming of the great and notable day of the Lord.**
> **And it shall come to pass that whoever calls on the name of the Lord shall be saved.**
>
> **Acts 2:17–21 (NKJV)**

What Must We Do?

The great and awesome day of the Lord is the rapture. The Bible says Christ will come like a thief in the night and take His Church.

We had a woman in our church in Australia, who had spent several years during World War II in a Nazi concentration camp. She had become ill and was lying on the floor one day, knowing she was about to die. Someone said to her, "Hold on. The Yanks are coming to set us free. They are stronger than our enemies! It won't be long."

Church, God is shouting to our sick and dying world, "Hold on. I'm coming. I'm sending all My people, black, white and brown—but they're not coming alone. I've also sent the Holy Ghost and power—together they are stronger than all your enemies combined."

The world is waiting to see a holy army marching through the cities coming to set them free. The Church must repent, stand boldly and walk in power before the world will join the ranks.

Folks, it's thirty seconds to midnight! Before Jesus raptures His Bride, HE WILL POUR OUT HIS SPIRIT!

He will confirm His Word with signs and wonders!

He will do it again!

The clock is ticking down!

Many will call upon the name of the Lord and be saved!

We will see revival!

God will flow through His Church manifesting His power!

Then the clock will strike midnight!

And the victorious Bride of Christ will ascend into Heaven...

We'll go out with a shout!

Do you know Jesus Christ as your personal Lord and Savior?

Although this was written as a prophetic message to the Church of Jesus Christ, it is possible that you have read this book and have never invited Jesus Christ to come into your heart.

The Bible says unless we are born again, we cannot see the Kingdom of God (John 3:3).

You can't be saved through Buddha; you can't be saved through Krishna; neither can you be saved through Mary, or by joining a church.

You can't be saved by belonging to the Baptist, Assembly of God, Catholic or New Beginnings churches.

You can only be saved by being born again through the blood of Jesus. We all must be born again because, "There is none righteous, no, not one" (Romans 3:10).

If you've never received Jesus Christ as your Lord and Savior, you can be born again right now by praying this prayer. Do not simply repeat words, but talk to your heavenly Father. Although He hates sin, I can assure you that He loves the sinner. Pray with me right now, but speak it to Jesus:

Father, I come to You in the name of Jesus. I know I am a sinner, and I'm sorry for those sins. I repent right now. I receive Jesus Christ as my Savior. And, Lord Jesus, I ask You to come into my heart and forgive me. Jesus, as You died for

me, starting today I'm going to live for You. I am forgiven. I am born again. I am a child of God. Amen.

Asking for repentance from God our Creator releases the supernatural dimension of our lives and opens the door for growth in God's Kingdom order.

If you have just received Jesus, find a church in your area preaching salvation and the undiluted power of God.

If you would like prayer or more information on Larry Huch Ministries or New Beginnings Christian Center in Portland Oregon, write to us at:

CALLED TO CONQUER MINISTRIES
P.O. Box 66700
Portland, Oregon 97290
(503) 256-6050

Notes

Chapter 1
1. "Fashionable or Forceful?" *Christian History.* Issue 26. Volume IX, No 2. 1990: 2.

Chapter 2
1. Barnes, Albert. *Barnes' Notes On The New Testament.* Grand Rapids: Kregel Publications, 1962: 21.

Chapter 3
1. Ostling, Richard N. "The Church Search." *Time Magazine.* 5 April 1993: 44–49.

Chapter 4
1. Strong, James. *Strong's Exhaustive Concordance Of The Bible.* Peabody: Hendrickson Publishers, 24.

2. *Merriam-Webster's Collegiate Dictionary.* Springfield: Merriam-Webster, Inc. 1993: 361.

Chapter 5
1. Strong, James. *Strong's Exhaustive Concordance Of The Bible.* Peabody: Hendrickson Publishers, 70.

Cassette-Tape Series Available through
CALLED TO CONQUER MINISTRIES

Any of the four–tape series can be ordered for $20 each plus $2 shipping and handling per one item. For each additional item, please add $ .50.

Send your order requests to:

NEW BEGINNINGS CHRISTIAN BOOKSTORE
P.O. Box 66700
Portland, OR 97290

(503) 256–6050
FAX: (503) 256–2287

THE FATHERHOOD OF GOD

Pastor Larry Huch clearly explains who we are *through* God and who we are *in* God. We are joint–heirs with Christ Jesus. The heavenly Father desires to have a dynamic relationship with all His children. This inspiring message will release your walk with God into new dimensions.

RENEWING THE SPIRIT OF YOUR MIND

Our thoughts and words are creative spiritual forces. In this series, Pastor Larry Huch illustrates the power of the words we speak and our thought patterns. Whatsoever a man thinks, so he is (Proverbs 23:7). We all have the choice to speak and think success into our daily lives and into our relationship with the Lord. This motivational series will inspire you to rethink your words. Whosoever guards his mouth and heart, keeps his soul from trouble (Proverbs 21:23).

REVERSE THE CURSE

The Bible says God's people are destroyed for their lack of knowledge (Hosea 4:6). One of Satan's greatest strategies is to bind us with generational curses. Family curses are responsible for untold suffering, poverty and spiritual defeat. Pastor Huch releases the realization that we have all authority and power to reverse all curses and cast them back into the pit of hell!

KINGDOM PRINCIPLES ON FINANCES

Pastor Huch demonstrates kingdom keys to unlocking biblical prosperity. God says He has given His Children the power to gain wealth so He may establish His covenant (Deuteronomy 9:9). God wants His children blessed so they can be a blessing to others. This tape series is excellent for everyone seeking answers on God's financial success plan for His children.

Introducing Tiz Huch's newest book
God's Call to Women of the 90's
A bold, vital yet distinctly feminine role in the Body of Christ

The world is entering into the greatest outpouring of God's Spirit, power and anointing in history.

Although women have notoriously struggled with their identity in the Body of Christ, they have a vital part to play. This book teaches each woman how to find her distinct role in the 90's and her purpose in the Body of Christ. Tiz Huch explains how to:

- discover your particular gifts and callings.
- incorporate your gifts into everyday life.
- conquer fear, depression, unforgiveness and other destructive emotions and habits.
- become efficient and productive in your personal life.
- ignite your feminine fire of zeal, power and boldness without becoming overbearing and masculine.
- advance into the fullness of the destiny God has intended for *you*.

This book is a powerhouse of experiences, real-life stories, spiritual insight and wisdom that will change your life forever.

It speaks to women of every age—married or single.

It addresses women from every walk of life or ministry.

It can be applied to any stage of Christianity (newly converted to seasoned ministries).

It covers both the practical and spiritual issues of life and ministry.

If you desire more of God and more out of life, this book is absolutely for *You!*

To order Tiz's newest book or for more information on tapes, videos or bookings, please call or write:

NEW BEGINNINGS CHRISTIAN BOOKSTORE
P.O. Box 66700
Portland, OR 97290
(503) 256–6050

Elizabeth (Tiz) Huch is co-pastor of New Beginnings Christian Center in Portland, Oregon with her husband, Larry. She is also the founder and director of "Women of Excellence," a ministry challenging and teaching women across the country to rise to their full potential and destiny. She is a frequent speaker at conferences and seminars and the producer of several successful tape and video series on spiritual warfare, marriage, womanhood, the family and the dynamics of victorious Christian living.